P9-CIT-274

SWEDEN

BONECHI

Concept: Casa Editrice Bonechi - *Project and picture research:* Monica Bonechi
Graphics, layout and cover: Manuela Ranfagni - *Make-up:* Federica Balloni
Texts: Patrizia Fabbri - *English translation:* Julia Hanna Weiss
Editing: Federica Balloni, Patrizia Fabbri - *Drawings:* Stefano Benini

© Copyright by Casa Editrice Bonechi, Via Cairoli 18/b – Florence – Italy
E-mail: bonechi@bonechi.it

*Team work. All rights reserved. No part of this publication may be reproduced, stored or transmitted in any form or by any means,
whether electronic, chemical or mechanical, including photocopying, recording or cinema, television or radio, or by any information storage or retrieval system
without prior written permission from the publisher.
The cover, layout and all work by the* Casa Editrice Bonechi *graphic artists featured in this book are covered by international copyright.*

Printed in Italy by Centro Stampa Editoriale Bonechi, *Sesto Fiorentino.*

The photographs are the property of the Casa Editrice Bonechi *Archives.*

Other contributors: Francesco Giannoni*: pages 23 above left, 48, 49, 82 below, 84 below, 85 above.*
Ina Agency Press*: pages 4-5, 18 above, 21 below, 27 below, 28 below, 29 above and centre, 31 above, centre and below left, 34 above left and below, 36 above and below, 3
7, 42 below, 47 below right, 58 above and centre, 59 centre, 60 above, 61 above, 63 centre, 68 below, 70 centre and below, 72 below, 75, 83 below left, 88 below,
89, 91 below, 92, 93 above right and below, 94 centre and below.*
NordicPhotos / IMS Bildbyrå / Mira Bildarkiv*: pages 8-9, 19, 20-21 below, 21 above and centre, 22-23 below, 25, 26, 27 above, 28 above,
29 below right and left, 30, 31 below right, 32-33, 34 above right, 38-39, 40 above right and below, 41 above left, 42 centre, 43, 44 centre, 50-51, 52-53, 54 below, 55 above, 56, 57, 58-59
below, 59 above, 60-61 below, 61 centre, 62 centre, 62-63, 63 above, 65, 66-67, 68 above, 69 below, 73 above, 76 below, 77 below,
78 above and below left, 79, 80-81, 82-83 above, 83 below right, 85 above, 86-87, 88 above, 90, 91 above, 93 above left, 94-95, 95.*
Photographs pages 3, 7 below, 32 below, 33 below, 46 below, 77 above: *courtesy of* Ultraforlaget.

*The publisher will be grateful for information concerning the sources of photographs without credits
and will be pleased to acknowledge them in future editions.*

ISBN 978-88-476-1800-8
Internet: www.bonechi.com

INTRODUCTION

In addition to being the biggest country on the Scandinavian peninsula – and one of the largest in all Europe – Sweden is a fascinating mix of wild, uncontaminated nature, deeply rooted old traditions, a vibrant cultural life and one of the most civilized, democratic populations in the whole world. Sweden extends over an area of 450,000 square kilometers between the region of Skåne in the south and Lapland in the north; the northernmost part of Sweden is a meeting point of three countries: Sweden, Norway and Finland. In fact, it borders with Norway on the west, with Finland on the northeast, the North Sea on the southwest, the Baltic Sea on the southeast and with the Gulf of Bothnia on the east. Notwithstanding its size, Sweden's population is a mere 9 million and it is concentrated in the South and Center. Stockholm, the capital, is home to about one and a half million people, while Lapland, the great northern region is almost completely uninhabited.

Geography and Climate

The landmass known as Sweden was formed about two and a half billion years ago, but it was during the glacial period that the composite conformation of the land developed.

The north is characterized mainly by the Scandinavian Mountain Chain: the main peak is Mount Kebnekaise (2,111 meters). Going south, the mountains make way for the large plateaus formed by repeated shifts in the glaciers and hilly areas that gradually slope down to the coasts. In the center are the great lakes, proof that the area was once below sea level. The many rivers are an important source of hydroelectric power, in addition to providing transportation for the logging and fishing industries. Mitigated by the Gulf Stream, Sweden's climate is temperate, but can vary considerably according to the region. Winters are long and harsh, summers short and intense, and while there are four quite distinct seasons in the south, up north it can snow even in the middle of August!

In the area above the Arctic Circle, the sun does not rise at all during winter. But in summer, from mid-May to mid-July, the "midnight sun" shines 24 hours a day.

Typical features of the Swedish climate are wind and rain. And perhaps this is why weather is a favorite topic for discussion among Swedes who, for their vacations prefer Spain, Italy and all those countries which, in addition to great cultural traditions offer mild temperatures and warm sunshine. This preference extends to Swedish homes that are decorated in warm tones, with lots of wood, decorated tiles and pastel colors to create a cozy, welcoming atmosphere.

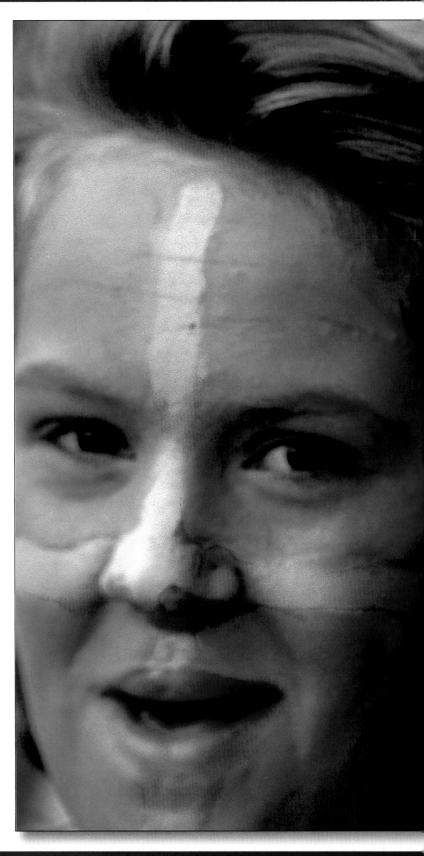

The Swedish people love nature and the outdoors, traditions, celebrations and a drink with friends. They are charming and extroverted, hospitable, creative and always open to learning about different cultures.

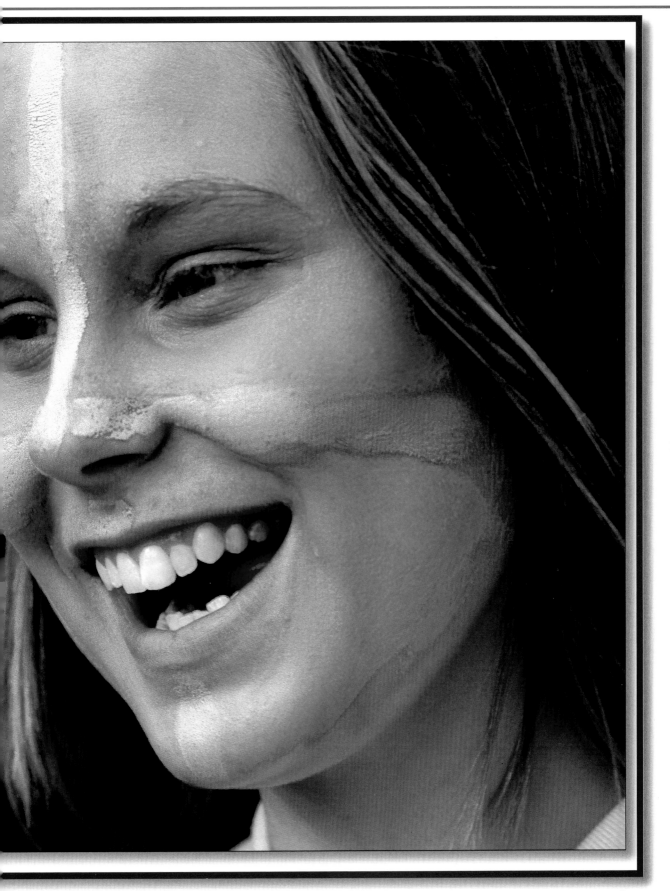

Historical notes

Sweden's history began around the year 12,000 B.C. when the thick sheet of ice that covered the whole country gradually began to melt leaving the southern portion uncovered. That was when the nomadic hunters and fishermen began their explorations; they were supplanted only in the IV millennium B.C. by stable populations who farmed, raised livestock and lived in villages. The earliest pictorial evidence dates from the Bronze Age (1500 B.C.): splendid, perfectly conserved cave paintings of hunting scenes or daily life. It was the Roman historian Tacitus who told about the early inhabitants of Sweden in his book Germania, and he described them as being of Germanic origin. Among these were the Svear who, though defeated by the Goths, gave the country its name Sverige – Sweden – and established their political and religious capital at Uppsala.

Sweden's centuries of isolation were interrupted during the Era of the Vikings (700-1000 A.D.). The Vikings were navigators; much of their history is a mystery and even their name has not been definitively interpreted. Recent studies, however, reveal that the Vikings had a great and complex civilization. In addition to being daring navigators, they produced fine poets, artists and explorers. Skilled sailors with their agile ships (the famous drakkar) it seems that they used spar – a mineral that polarizes sunlight – as a navigational tool. Established mostly in the area around what is now Stockholm, they had contacts with Russia, Constantinople, Great Britain and Ireland and opened numerous trading routes. Gradually, as their relationships with Germany and England intensified, missionaries began traveling to Sweden strengthening the influence of Christianity which, by the XII century was the dominant religion after King Olof Skötkonung was baptized in 1008. The

country's political and economic power also strengthened during the same period when Finland was annexed and the capital, Stockholm was founded. In 1389 Margareta, Queen of Denmark and Norway, assumed the Swedish crown and united the Scandinavian kingdoms. The diverse interests of the people, however, led to a series of insurrections and rebellions that culminated in a terrible event during the reign of Christian II of Denmark: he subdued the Swedish resistance with the "bloodbath" of 1520. Sweden did, however, achieve independence thanks to Gustav Eriksson Vasa who roused the entire country to rebellion and brought an end to Danish rule. Gustav Vasa was elected king of Sweden and from that time on the monarchy became hereditary. It was the Vasa Dynasty, that reigned for 150 years that introduced Protestantism, making Lutheranism the dominant faith. In the XVII century, during the reign of Gustav II Adolf (1611-1632) Sweden became the most powerful country in Europe and conquered entire regions of Russia and Poland. Gustav II Adolf was succeeded by his daughter, Kristina, who was crowned in 1644. She was an enlightened ruler who gave a major boost to Scandinavian cultural life. During the reigns of her successors, Sweden obtained Scania and the southern provinces as well as parts of the Baltic and Germany from Denmark. This period of power ended upon the death of Karl XII in 1718, the great warrior who was defeated by Peter the Great at Poltava. The country lost many of its possessions and was weakened both economically and politically. It was then that the ruling class took the reins by limiting the monarch's power and entrusting government of the country to the Council appointed by the Diet or Parliament (Riksdag). The advent of Gustav III, revived the monarchy's power and gave rise to a true "enlightened despotism." But when the king was assassinated by a noble, his successors did not prove to be as skilled and Sweden went into a period of decline until the Marshal of France Jean-Baptiste Bernadotte was elected king and took the throne as Karl XIV Johan. His descendants continue to reign today. Under Karl XIV Johan Sweden defeated Denmark and annexed Norway which only regained its independence in 1905. It was in the middle of the nineteenth century that the foundations were laid for the very democratic welfare system of today's Sweden – and yet, at the time it was a poor country with a high rate of emigration. Sweden maintained neutrality during the two World Wars, and in the roughly sixty years that it has been in power, the Social Democratic party implemented the many social reforms that have given Sweden one of the most efficient welfare systems in the world.

THE ROYAL FAMILY

The Bernadotte dynasty that currently reigns in Sweden has its roots in southern France. It was Jean-Baptiste Bernadotte, son of Henry, the procurator of Pau who brought the family to glory, First as a general and then marshal of the French Empire under Napoleon and ambassador to Vienna in 1798 he earned the respect of the Swedes when, as governor of the Hanseatic cities (1807-1808) he showed great humanity towards the Scandinavian prisoners along with obvious talents as a administrator. And so, Karl XIII who was childless, with the consent of Parliament, designated Jean-Baptiste Bernadotte as the perfect heir apparent to the throne. In 1818 he was crowned Karl XIV Johan, king of Sweden and Norway. His descendant, Carl XVI Gustaf has been on the throne since 1973, with his wife, Queen Silvia who has given him three wonderful children, Crown Princess Victoria, heir to the throne, Prince Carl Philip and Princess Madeleine.

The royal family, is well-loved by the subjects, both for the democratic modernity it has nurtured while respecting traditions and for its image of tranquil harmony. The members of the family live in the splendid *Drottningholm Palace,* even though the king and queen discharge their many official duties in the huge rooms of the Royal Palace in *Gamla Stan.*

A country with a history counted in millennia: opposite page, a Runic stone with typical carvings and a replica of an old Viking ship – unsurpassed mistress of the seas.
On this page, an official portrait of the reigning sovereign, King Carl XVI Gustaf with Queen Silvia.

STOCKHOLM

*D*efined as the "city between the waters," the "city between the bridges" or the "city on the island," Stockholm is an extraordinarily "livable" city, situated amidst green woods and the blue waters of the canals that divide it among the fourteen islands it has grown to encompass over the centuries. According to tradition, it was founded in the middle of the thirteenth century by Birger Jarl, regent for his son Valdemar, king of Sweden. Thanks to a succession of enlightened sovereigns the city grew into a true European cultural capital.

Today, with its extraordinary Nordic light, surrounded by deep blue, almost an enchanted place floating on the water, Stockholm is perhaps the only city in the world where it is possible to swim or fish anywhere: pollution is inexistent and the environment is so carefully protected that no heavy industry is allowed in the vicinity.

On the east it is lapped by the waves of the Baltic Sea and on the west by Lake Mälaren; the meeting of the waves and the lake's waters generate currents so strong that even salmon fishing is possible. Sailboats, rowboats, ferries and craft of all types are an integral part of the city's splendid panorama, as are the long bridges for motor vehicles that connect the extraordinary mosaic of its islands. The historic city center is ideal for walking, while in the outlying areas, the layouts and features of their buildings clearly reveal when they became part of Stockholm's urban fabric. And finally, the city has large, beautiful parks, green oases in the modern city as well as fine settings for musical and theatrical events with songs, ballets and folk dancing especially during great traditional Nordic holidays such as Midsummer and the Feast of St. Lucy.

Glimpses of the Stortorget: narrow little streets, colorful facades, distinctive frontons.

Stockholm, the famous *Vädersolstavlan* painting. The most outstanding of all, however, is to the left of the altar: *Saint George and the Dragon*, a sculptural group in oak wood and elk-horn carved by Berndt Notke between 1483 and 1489 commissioned by the regent Sten Sture who saved Stockholm from the eager and voracious expansion of the Danes.

Kungliga Slottet (Royal Palace)

Following the fire that destroyed the *Fortress of the Three Crowns* in 1697, Nicodemus Tessin the Younger was commissioned to build a new palace, befitting a European capital. The models were the great Italian palazzos, the style baroque and the objective a well-proportioned, symmetrical building around a large inner courtyard, with harmony of shape and a linear structure. The result was the splendid **Royal Palace**, one of the largest in all Europe with over 600 rooms, that is still used for its original purpose. It was completed by Tessin's son, Karl Gustav with the help of Carl Hårleman. The palace was inaugurated by King Adolf Fredrik, and it was decorated by the leading European artists of the period. The triumphal arch on the southern facade leads to the wing that hosts the immense *Hall of State* (*Rikssalen*), Hårleman's architectural masterpiece, where we can still admire the splendid chased silver *throne* (1650) made for Queen Kristina. This wing also houses the *Royal Chapel* and the **Treasury** that contains the crown jewels, including the crown that belonged to Erik XIV (1561). In the west wing are the **State Apartments** (*Representationsvåningen*), the oldest part of the palace, with its beautiful furnishings and splendid Gobelin tapestries. In this wing we can admire the *Antechamber of Queen Lovisa Ulrika* in the *Bernadotte Apartments* (which house a fine collection of Italian paintings), the rococo style of the *Bernadotte Apartments* and the enormous *Ballroom* (the "White Sea" because of its beautiful white walls). In the north wing in the *State Apartments* is the **Gustav**

The city's streets

When Stockholm was a flourishing port and a major trading center in close contact with the Hanseatic cities, the streets of *Gamla Stan* bustled with sailors, workers and stevedores, loyal clients of the hundreds of taverns that literally made fortunes. All this activity enlivened the two main (and oldest) streets in the district, *Österlånggatan* and *Västerlånggatan* which run towards the cathedral and the palace. Originally the first streets marked a rudimentary urban layout around the fortress, today they

abound with glittering store windows, cafés and restaurants.

Storkyrkan (Cathedral)

Near *Stortorget* stands the **cathedral**, on the highest point of *Stadsholmen* where Birger Jarl wanted Stockholm to have its church. Destroyed by a fire, it was replaced by a majestic basilica dedicated to Saint Nicholas and consecrated in 1306. This was the ancestor of today's cathedral with its Gothic interior that dates from the fourteenth century reconstruction. The baroque *facade* was built in the mid-eighteenth century by J. E. Carlberg to harmonize with the nearby Royal Palace. He also designed the *bell tower* (1743) the most visible feature of this cathedral that is squeezed between the houses of the old city center. The site of all official celebrations, the cathedral houses priceless treasures: from the *Silver Altar* (1650 ca.) to the *Royal Thrones*, designed by Nicodemus Tessin the Younger in 1684, to the *Pulpit* carved by Burchardt Precht in 1705, to the oldest (XVI century) view of

III's State Bedchamber and the baroque *Gallery of Karl XI*, one of the most magnificent, and biggest rooms in the entire palace. And finally, the eastern portion of the palace extends in two small wings which host the *Gustav III Antikmuseum* and the **Royal Armory** (*Livrustkammaren*), the oldest museum in Sweden, established in 1628 showcasing armor, carriages, weapons, original Swedish clothing and costumes. All the rooms in this extraordinary palace are, however, astounding for their magnificent design and lavish furnishings and decorations. Even the two grand *staircases*, on the east and west, respectively can rightfully be described as spectacular. They were designed by Tessin the Younger and built from Swedish marble and limestone. But when we speak of refinement and baroque opulence, nothing can compare with the extraordinary, light-filled

The elegant southern facade of the Royal Palace dominates the Slottsbacken; in the background the obelisk and the cathedral. Below, the magnificent silver throne that was built for Queen Kristina, and right the Royal Chapel.

Royal Chapel (*Slottskyrkan*) in the southern wing. This rococo chapel was built by Carl Hårleman to plans by Nicodemus Tessin the Younger.

Stadshuset (City Hall)

Stadshuset, the *City Hall*, is an impressive red brick building (eight million), surmounted by a massive tower topped with the three crowns of the Swedish coat of arms. Initially, the majestic, quadrilateral Stadshuset which almost recalls an old fortress, was designed with two courtyards (according to the typical layout of Italian Renaissance palaces), however, only one remained when construction was completed. The other was covered, and even though it has an airy staircase and portico that still reveal its intended purpose, it now is the splendid *Blå Hallen*, the **Blue Room** with marble floors and red brick walls. Even the interior of the Stadshuset holds other, extraordinary surprises. For example, upstairs, next door to and almost overshadowing the Blue Room as it flanks the balcony, is the *Gyllene Salen*, or **Golden Hall**. It was designed as a banquet hall and is decorated with Byzantine-inspired mosaics (the largest work of mosaics of modern times). The **Council Room**, where the City Council of Stockholm has it's meetings, with its sumptuous furnishings (the furniture was designed by Carl Malmsten, the upholstery by Maja Sjöström) and the extraordinary ceiling astounds with its majesty. However, on the topic of amazing achievements, the singular *Prinsens Galleri*, the **Gallery of the Prince**, is no less astonishing. It is used for official receptions, but is famous mainly for the lively frescoes of the shores of Stockholm with a scenic view of Lake Mälaren, by Prince Eugen, and elegantly framed by paired columns. Before leaving the Stockholm City Hall we should also stop at the interesting **museum** in the tower. The top of the tower (106 meters high) offers a stupendous view of the whole city.

Views of Stockholm's City Hall (seen on the left from Riddarholmen where some interesting sculptures are situated, such as Solbåten, a work in granite by Christer Berg dated 1966); above left, the terraces and gardens face out across the water; on the right, the brightly-lit Gilded Room, and the spectacular Blue Room; below, the golden statue of Birger Jarl, lying in the shade of a canopy on the east side of the tower.

THE NOBEL PRIZE

The Nobel Prize is given by the foundation established by the last will and testament of Alfred Nobel, who bequeathed a fortune estimated at the time (1896) as 31.5 million Swedish kronor. According to the terms of his will, each year the foundation would award five prizes of equal amount (the amount is determined on the basis of the foundation's income, and, it may shared by two or three individuals). The prizes would be given to those who, on an international level (in other words, it was not limited to Scandinavians) had done the most in terms of "services to mankind" in the fields of physics, chemistry, physiology or medicine, literature and peace. This last award, the most complex in political terms and therefore the one which most frequently has not been given, was conceived to honor the work of those who had favored brotherhood among peoples and the withdrawal of permanent armies. Starting in 1969 the Bank of Sweden has sponsored another prize in memory of Alfred Nobel: for economics.

THE NOBEL MEDALS

In addition to a considerable check, Nobel Prize winners also receive a certificate and a medal. On the obverse is a portrait of Alfred Nobel, while on the reverse are images that vary from prize to prize. Nature, symbolized by the goddess Isis rising from clouds, while the Spirit of Science lifts a veil from her face is on the physics and chemistry medals; the Spirit of Medicine, portrayed as a woman drawing water to quench the thirst of a sick child is on the physiology and medicine awards. A youth sitting in the shade of laurel tree while transcribing the song of a muse is the literature award; and three men concluding a pact of brotherhood are on the Peace Prize. Then there is economics prize given by the Bank of Sweden. This medal, too, bears a portrait of Alfred Nobel and on the reverse side the symbol of the Royal Academy of Sciences. The first four medals were designed by Erik Lindberg, the fifth by Gustav Vigeland and the sixth by Gunvor Svensson-Lundkvist.

to Gauguin. These are displayed in the spacious gallery on the second floor. And there are 500,000 *drawings*, as well as the largest collection of *porcelain* in Scandinavia (many pieces are Italian and date from the XV and XVI centuries and are located in the first floor rooms), and an outstanding collection of *tapestries* (first floor) from Brussels, Tournai and Oudenarde ranging from the fifteenth to the twentieth century. Modern Swedish design and the *applied arts* are also well represented. Of the countless items of inestimable artistic and historical value we must mention the *coronation cloak worn by Gustav II Adolf*, and a late XV century Italian polychrome relief of a *Deposition*. On the ground floor of the *Nationalmuseum* are a large auditorium and spacious rooms for temporary exhibits which offer opportunities for discovery and learning.

Vasamuseet

For three years, starting in 1625, hundreds of workers, carpenters, cabinet makers, carvers, smiths, rope-makers and laborers worked ceaselessly, using tons of oak to fulfill what was perhaps a somewhat presumptuous dream of King Gustav II Adolf. He wanted a gigantic man of war, the biggest ever, with 50 meter masts, 64 guns and hundreds of gilded, painted statues. All the dockyards of *Skeppsholmen* and shipyards of *Blasieholmen* worked on the project while Europe fearfully followed its progress. The big day arrived on 10 August 1628.

Watched by the curious and admired by the people of Stockholm gathered along the shores of the islands, this marvel of nautical technology, the pride of the king and all Sweden that had cost so much and was to give such satisfaction, could finally be launched. The royal vessel, a mighty warship weighed anchor and set off towards the open sea.

It had gone barely 1300 meters when, just off the *Kastellholmen* shore, as soon as the wind began to fill the sails, it began to list and then, quickly sank with all its guns and a crew of hundreds. The king, who was on the Prussian battlefields, got the disastrous news two weeks later. Was it due to a design error, the ship's lack of stability, the king's excessive pride? In any case, it was a terrible shock. The king ordered a full – and harsh – investigation with many people accused but none found guilty, maybe

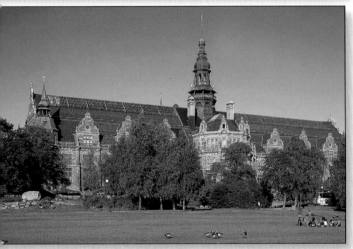

Nationalmuseum

This important Swedish museum occupying three floors of the large building overlooking the *Norrström* and offers an incredible collection of artworks. In fact, we can admire over 16,000 *paintings* and *sculptures* by the greatest talents in the world, from Bronzino to Veronese, from Tiepolo to Canaletto, from Rembrandt to Rubens, from Van Dyck to Brueghel, from Goya to Ribera, from Delacroix to Renoir, from Monet to Cézanne

Above, a sunny view that highlights the harmony and symmetry of the facade of the Nationalmuseum; top, the Renaissance-style castle built at the end of the XIX century to provide a suitable home for the Nordiska Museet; right, the original appearance of the Vasa Museum, built around the wreck of the royal ship from which it takes the name.

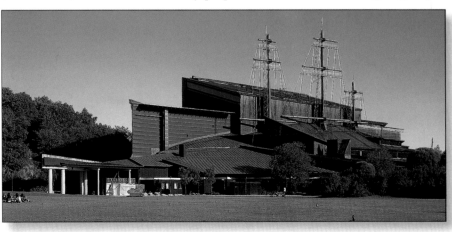

because it was simply too difficult to attribute the real blame: the king's excessive expectations that could not be disappointed. It was the death of a dream and the birth of a legend. A legend which after centuries of attempts to raise the ship with its precious cargo, finally surfaced to become reality in 1961. The ship was carefully restored and protected to become a truly extraordinary museum, literally built around the ship with the tall masts protruding majestically from the roof. All the micro-climatic conditions to guarantee the perfect conservation of the ship were carefully prepared. Every year hundreds of thousands of visitors walk through galleries on the seven floors of the museum to contemplate the 69 meter long "Vasa" from every angle. Replicas and scale models, films and archeological finds tell the story of the ship, the building techniques, the glories of Swedish nautical skill and, of course, how it was raised.

Nordiska Museet

The museum is housed in a nineteenth century Renaissance-style castle designed by Isak Gustaf Clason. It was ordered by Artur Hazelius who also established the *Skansen*, and started the collections; the museum was opened in 1907. The very popular *Nordiska Museet*, with more than 1.5 million objects on display, its settings (including the famous table set for a lavish seventeenth century banquet), and its galleries offer a detailed overview of Sweden's life, culture, traditions and crafts in the past 500 years. Not far from here, another museum, the *Junibacken* is dedicated to more recent Swedish traditions.

Extraordinary pictures of the "Vasa" and its museum.

Riksdagshuset seen from the sea.

Helgeandsholmen

This is the smallest of the islands around *Gamla Stan*, bathed by the waters of the *Norrström*, and connected to the *Stadsholmen* by two bridges. The **Riksdagshuset** dominates the western portion of *Helgeandsholmen*. Construction was begun in 1888 to plans by Aron Johansson and was completed around 1906, first housing the two and, subsequently single-chamber Parliament. It was enlarged and updated several times and today the Parliament building flanks the **Medeltidsmuseet** which is devoted to Medieval Stockholm. The museum owes its origins to important items that were unearthed beneath the parliament when

Sailing craft of all kinds, from boats to yachts and ferries, crowd the Strandvägen, a typical example of Stockholm's lively marine life and busy canals.

excavations, to build an underground parking facility, were underway. These finds were so interesting, that the museum was built instead of the garage.

Östermalm

Crisscrossed by long, wide avenues, such as the elegant *Strandvägen* which flanks the canal leading to the *Djurgårdsbrunnsviken*, *Östermalm* is distinguished by large, stately late-nineteenth and early twentieth century buildings commissioned by the city's wealthiest families of the period. Their majestic facades overlook the many boats anchored in the canal, and some are the headquarters of interesting institutions. One of the most noteworthy is the **Kungliga Dramatiska Teatern** (the Royal Theater of Dramatic Arts) at *Nybroplan*, at the north-west end of *Strandvägen*. It is housed in a typical art deco building, of Viennese inspiration, with a white marble facade and is surmounted by statues created by Carl Milles The theater, which was opened in 1908, is famous for its lavishly decorated interior as well as its fine performances. All around there is greenery, with large plazas (from the *Östermalmstorg* to the *Karlaplan*) where even the parks (like the *Nobelparken*) overlook the water, and outdoor activities from walking to bicycling to boating are a delight.

However, most important museum in the *Östermalm* district is the **Historiska Museet**. Dedicated to the Prehistoric, Viking and Medieval periods of these lands, the museum was inaugurated in 1943. Here we can admire one of the richest collections of prehistoric gold and silver jewels as well as unique items and Viking ornaments (which were divided into pieces and used as money), displayed in the magnificent *Gold Room* that was opened to the public in 1994. Many of these precious objects were found during the nineteenth century on farmlands and the owners, admirably, returned them to the Swedish State.

Södermalm

The island of *Södermalm* presents itself with a picturesque avenue, the *Söder Mälarstrand*, which runs along the southern side of Lake Mälaren and offers a lovely view of the nearby islands, in particular, *Kungsholmen, Riddarholmen* and *Gamla Stan*. However, the view is even more fascinating from the **Katarinahissen** platform. The elevator, which went into service in 1883 and was modernized several times, rises to a height of 38 meters and offers a 360° view of the city as well as easy access to the just as panoramic *Mosebacke terrace*. *Katarinahissen* dominates one of the island's main squares, *Södermalmstorg* which is not far from the **Stockholms Stadsmuseum** (the museum dedicated to the city's history) is housed in a beautiful Baroque building designed by Nicodemus Tessin the Younger (1680). We reach this plaza via the elaborate **Slussen** bridge which connects the island to **Gamla Stan**. The bridge was built by using a 1637 weir which served to compensate for the difference in height between Lake Mälaren and Saltsjön Bay. Going further inland we will see other interesting buildings such as the elegant **Katarina kyrka** church with its Baroque dome, built by Jean de Vallée. It was completed in 1690 and then beautifully restored after the devastating fire of 1990, and the austere **Södra Teatern**, built on the *Mosebacke Torg* in 1859 to plans by Johan Fredrik Åbom. However, the most fascinating aspect of this island is the maze of streets flanked by old houses, wooden cottages and the charming homes in *Fjällgatan* that take us back to the olden days when, between the seventeenth and nineteenth century, *Södermalm* was thought to be a witches' haven. It was also the seat of severe courts and the site of executions.

The elegant building that houses Stockholm's Stadsmuseum and below, the sophisticated profile of the modern Katarinahissen.

Norrmalm

Leaving little *Helgeandsholmen* via the *Norrbro* bridge we come to the large *Norrmalm* district. We cross the vast **Gustav Adolfs Torg**, a pretty plaza, designed by Nicodemus Tessin the Younger, with the *statue* of the great King Gustav II Adolf. One of the outstanding buildings – because of its essential architectural linearity – skirting the plaza is the **Dansmuseet**, the only institute of its kind in the world: the only museum and research center devoted entirely to dance. It is no coincidence then that the building stands next door to the **Kungliga Operan,** the *Royal Opera House* overlooking the east side of the plaza. Built at the end of the nineteenth century over the site of a theater dating from the reign of Gustav III (it was opened on 30 September 1792) it was designed by Axel Anderberg who had it lavishly furnished and decorated, in perfect visual harmony with its two illustrious neighbors, the Royal Palace and the Parliament building.

Behind the theater is one of the most beautiful green areas. It is a favorite of Stockholm's residents: the **Kungsträdgården** that was created in the XV century. Originally it was a private park and sort of a vegetable garden for the royal family. Today it hosts festivals, music and dance concerts and street artists. On the south side it is bounded by the commanding *statue of Karl XII* made by Johan Molin in 1868; from here, long streets flanked by stores go north towards the heart of the city between big, modern buildings. Continuing north we will have the opportunity to admire the symbols of modern Stockholm: the five unmistakable skyscrapers on the Sveavägen that marked the beginning of a new urban development program. After the projects in the 'twenties and 'thirties, by the middle of the twentieth century the program was created to deal with the city's rapid unstoppable growth as the population had surpassed one million and it radically transformed a large part of Norrmalm. It was already home to the **Kungsgatan** (one of Stockholm's major business streets, designed in 1915 by Sven Wallander based on models of American streets), which boasts the two oldest skyscrapers in the city, the **Kungstornen** (*Royal Towers*). This area is also known for the **Hötorget,** with its colorful fruit and vegetable market, and for the neoclassical **Konserthuset** (*Concert Hall*). This is where the Nobel Prizes are awarded every year. However, there is another plaza that symbolizes the modern soul of Norrmalm: **Sergels Torg,** dedicated to one of Sweden's greatest sculptors (Johan Tobias Sergel, 1740-1814), with a glass *fountain* by Edvin Öhrström (1974). It faces Peter Celsing's **Kulturhuset** (built 1966-1970), a futuristic cultural center with exhibition rooms, theaters, auditoriums, conference rooms and a very rich library.

From the top: the sombre outline of the building that houses the Dansmuseet with the equestrian statue of Gustav II Adolf in front; a view of the elegant Opera House; the twin buildings of the Kungstornen on Kungsgatan; the futuristic Sergels Torg with the crystal fountain and the Kulturhuset with its remarkable glass facade.

DROTTNINGHOLMS SLOTT

Sweden too has its "Versailles." It is located on the island of Lovön in Lake Mälaren: since 1981 **Drottningholm Palace** has been the permanent residence of the Royal Family. Built in the XVI century it was razed to the ground by fire. It was only in the mid-seventeenth century, under orders from Hedvig Eleonora, wife of Karl X that the architects Nicodemus Tessin the Elder and Nicodemus Tessin the Younger constructed the existing palace which is a fine mix of international and Swedish, or Gustavian, Baroque styles, and the French Baroque park. Around the end of the eighteenth century an English garden surrounded the park which was embellished with a *Chinese Pavilion* and a wooden *Theater* (1766) that still conserves its original structure and decorations. In fact, it may be the only theater in the world that has remained unchanged for 200 years, and that includes its stage machinery, the back-drops and the furnishings. It is for this reason that in 1992 UNESCO declared the theater, as well as the Drottningholm Palace and Chinese Pavilion as "world heritage sites," a designation given to but few places or buildings of particular importance in the history of mankind.

Drottingholms Slott: this impressive castle on the island of Lovon is reflected in the waters of the Lake Malaren. Above, a beautiful military encampment in the park of Drottningholm.

MILLESGÅRDEN

Northwest of Stockholm, connected to the mainland by a bridge, the island of *Lidingö* is home to the highly original **museum** dedicated to the works of the Swedish sculptor Carl Milles (1875-1955). Set up in the artist's home and park, decorated with Pompeian mosaics and donated to Sweden in 1936, the museum is a rare example of a perfect balance between nature and art. The rooms and panoramic terraces are decorated with many sculptures and fountains by Carl Milles. Several are copies of originals which are on exhibit abroad, mainly in the United States where Milles lived for several years and acquired considerable fame. But this fact, does not diminish the statues' charm – such as the slim figures of the *Musical Angels* balanced on tall columns, the severe *Hand of God*, or the cheerful mythological figures on the *Fountain of Aganippe* on *Olga's Terrace* – named for the artist's beloved wife who did a fine portrait of him. Inside the museum-house we can enjoy Milles's personal collection of approximately 200 ancient Greek and Roman pieces plus items from every era and country. Like the garden, the museum is open all year.

Left, one of the works by Milles displayed in the garden that surrounds the house of the artist. Inside, in the Music Room, is the organ which Leopold Mozart, father of Wolfgang Amadeus, played as well as works by Donatello, Canaletto, Pissarro and Utrillo.

SKÄRGÅRDEN

The more than 24,000 islands comprising the Archipelago facing Stockholm, the *Skärgården*, the "garden on the rocks" are favorite destinations for vacations and weekend excursions for many of the city's natives. Easily reached by ferry or taxiboats, or by land and private craft (one family out of every three in Sweden owns some sort of boat) the islands and islets immediately reveal their rich and varied vegetation and brilliant colors. They are also home to charming towns that have attracted many artists and writers over the centuries. August Strindberg used to spend his vacations at *Dalarö*, which is famous for its fishing villages. Carl Larsson and Anders Zorn portrayed the lights and atmosphere of these places in their paintings. Once used to defend Stockholm from enemies arriving by sea, some of these islands still conserve traces of their original purpose. At *Vaxholm* – one of the most popular towns of the archipelago – for example, there is still a XVI century fortress which has been transformed into a museum featuring Sweden's military defensive systems over the centuries. But the greatest attraction, in addition to the beaches and sports facilities, are the old wooden houses. The elegant carvings that decorate the eaves, verandas and windows create a most picturesque effect.

Right and below, views of the archipelago of Stockholm, with a wealth of beaches, rocky outcrops and history, as well as traditional little houses and beautiful scenery and also home to an amazing variety of flora and fauna.

LAKE MÄLAREN
AND SIGTUNA

Lake Mälaren is a large lacustrine basin fed by many rivers. It is the third biggest lake in Sweden that extends as far as Stockholm. Its jagged contours, thousands of deep coves, and hundreds of islets make it an absolute "must see" for all visitors. It is here on the **island of Birka** (*Björkö*) that a French monk began preaching the Gospel and evangelizing the local population in the IX century. Evidence of the area's impor-

Left, a view of Lake Mälaren.
Below, Gripsholms Slott, at Mariefred.

tance from a religious standpoint is the interesting city of **Sigtuna** founded by Olof Skötkonung that was also the first capital of Sweden. It rises on the shores of Lake Mälaren and until the Middle Ages was an important point of reference for the Christian faith. This was helped by the fact that it was easily reached by boats directly from the Baltic Sea, of which Lake Mälaren was a deep bay.

Today it conserves many important signs of its historic role including XII century stone *churches*, ruins of ancient *monasteries* as well as lovely wooden homes and the *Town Hall* built in the local style. There are also the ruins of many Medieval churches including the *Church of St. Olof*, and the Dominican *Church of St. Maria klosterkyrkan* dating from the XIII century.

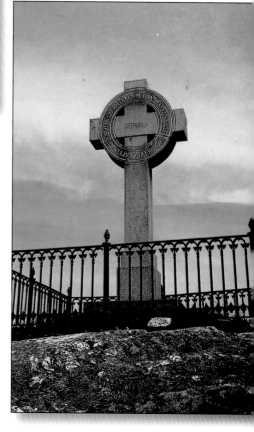

Right, the cross of Ansgar, evidence of the region's ancient spiritual character. Above right, the chapel dedicated to the French monk Ansgar, at Birka. Above left, a runic stone found at Mariefred.

UPPSALA

When thousands of students roam through the city's streets on Walpurgis Night, the eve of the Feast of St. Walpurga, 30 April, - wearing their white-topped caps, it is hard to believe that they are enrolled in the oldest university of all Scandinavia. The **University of Uppsala** is a national monument, founded in 1477, and a major cultural institution, located just 60 km from Stockholm.

The city that comprises a modern and an old district, known as *Gamla Uppsala* was an important religious and political center from the days of the Vikings. Its beautiful **cathedral** (built in the XIII century, but only consecrated in 1435) is still the seat of the Archbishopric of Sweden.

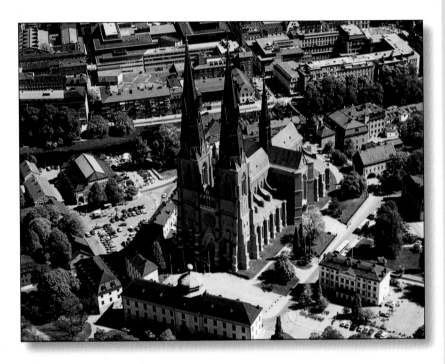

A LONG AND LASTING LOVE OF NATURE: CARL VON LINNÉ

We can call him Carl Nilsson, Carl von Linné, Carolus Linnaeus or simply Linneaus. If it is true that for Swedes a beloved child has many names, this son of Sweden has a very special place in the hearts of his compatriots. Linneaus is one of the figures who made some of the greatest contributions to Swedish and world science in the eighteenth century with his studies of plants and living organisms. His love of travel and careful observation of all parts of creation, and his sensitivity to natural cycles make him a point of reference in the lives of Swedes even today.

His treatise, *Systema Naturae*, first published in 1735, was the result of a careful, systematic study of the living world, based on rules of observation and denomination, through which he classified nature's three kingdoms.

At Uppsala, where Linneaus was professor of Medicine and Botany, there are many places commemorating him. At number 27 on *Svartbäcksgatan* is the *house* where he lived with his family for 35 years: today it is a museum. Here we can still admire the *botanical gardens* that he himself laid out in 1747 and which currently host 1300 floral species.

An unusual view of Gamla Uppsala on the site of an early Viking settlement. Right, the historic center of Uppsala dominated by the majestic cathedral.

Facing page, several views of Uppsala: left, the majestic cathedral where the kings were crowned; below right, the sixteenth century castle; below left, the University whose students enliven the city's atmosphere.

DESIGN

A country that is jealous of its traditions yet modern, in love with technology and the avant-garde, Sweden has linked its name and fame to a very particular – and peculiar – art and expressive form: design. Every year in February Stockholm hosts a design fair, and in Sweden, a land of designers and architects, the word achieves its broadest meaning. Design, in Sweden means modern interpretations of furnishing, lighting, murals, building and even a city's appearance (it is no accident that Stockholm has earned the nickname of "the trendiest city on the planet"), hotels with innovative rooms, railways, subway stations and the big residential neighborhoods. And yet, Swedish design is not just for the "large scale". It comes across most convincingly even in details: a lighting fixture, a chair, a box, a yogurt container or a window, which in Sweden, the home of design, are extraordinarily different and more elegant than anywhere else in the world.

ÖREBRO

Örebro, a city that played a major role in Sweden's history is the capital of the small province of Närke, south of Dalarna. The *castle*, originally a watchtower built by Birger Jarl in the XIII century hosted many sovereigns, and during the XV century Danish occupation it was a place of refuge for many heroes of Swedish independence. In each century Örebro was the scene of important events or resolutions: in 1347 the Parliament ratified the first common law, in 1436 it became the seat of the Estates General; in 1522 Gustav Vasa's armies took control of the city and seven years later it was there that the Lutheran Reformation was approved. In 1617 the first parliamentary rules were issued there, and finally in 1818 it was at Örebro that the French marshal Jean-Baptiste Bernadotte, the founder of the current reigning dynasty, was elected king of Sweden as Karl XIV Johan.

In addition to the castle which, notwithstanding many restorations, has conserved its sixteenth century appearance, the city has a modern landmark as well, the 58 meter high modern "*Svampen*" tower known as the "mushroom."

Above, a picturesque shot of the city at twilight over Lake Hjälmaren and below, the impressive bulk of the historic Örebro Slott surrounded by wide moats.

MÅRBACKA

One of the beautiful and popular tour-ist destinations in Värmland prov-ince is the valley that stretches from north to south along the picturesque **Lake Fryken** which is divided into two separate basins. Here, amidst lush forests, fine little harbors and uncontaminated nature, is the small, but charming *country house* of Mår-backa, birthplace of the area's most famous daughter, Selma Lagerlöf.

The birthplace of the famous writer Selma Lagerlöf and right, her desk and books.

SELMA LAGERLÖF

Born at Mårbacka in 1858 in a country house surrounded by greenery, Selma Lagerlöf maintained close ties to her childhood home even though destiny led her onto the paths of history. This sensitive, cultured lady soon took her place on the international literary scene and was the first woman ever to receive the Nobel Prize for literature (1909). Many of her works, from *The Gösta Berlings Saga* (1891) to *Tales of a Manor* (1899) draw their strength and charm from the descriptions of the atmosphere and beauties of her birthplace that she made both famous and eternal. It was thanks to the success of her books that Selma Lagerlöf was able to buy back the family home that had been sold upon her father's death, and where she returned to live. After she died (1940) she was buried in the nearby cemetery of Östra Ämstervik, while her home, filled with memories and mementoes became the property of the state.

CENTRAL SWEDEN

The geographic center of Sweden is also the true "heart" of the country, where old traditions have been preserved through the centuries and where the residents have always maintained a great respect for their history.

This area is the province of *Dalarna*, which literally means "The Valleys," a place of enchanting landscapes, as well as great cultural and ethnographic interest. The northernmost part is mountainous, and it was here that between the XV and XVI centuries that the people banded together against the Danes for the cause of Swedish independence. It is here, one of the most beautiful areas from the environmental and landscape viewpoints - around **Lake Siljan**, that folk traditions have been conserved most jealously. On holidays the people wear regional dress and listen to traditional music or attend exquisite ceremonies such as the "church-boats" that leads the faithful to worship in July.

But, it is mainly for the *Feast of Saint John the Baptist*, or *Midsummer* (celebrated on the Saturday closest to 24 June) that the region's multifaceted character is expressed to the full. "Maypoles" decorate the entire area and sleep is out of the question, as the night is spent in singing, dancing and feasting.

Some of the towns along the shores of Lake Siljan clearly manifest the area's features. Along with *Mora*, the birthplace of the painter Anders Zorn, we must mention *Nusnäs* where it seems that time has stopped. It was here – and it is no accident - that today, like a century ago, the Olsson family makes the *Dala horses* – the wooden horses of Dalarna, that are true symbols of Sweden.

Dalarna is truly an enchanted corner of Sweden. Above, a glimpse of its magnificent natural settings. Below, Lake Siljan. Opposite page: traditions are still very much alive in this land: above, a Maypole with Lake Siljan in the background. In the frame highlights of the Midsummer Festival.

MIDSUMMER NIGHT'S FEAST

The main, and most outstanding festival of the warm season is *Feast of Saint John the Baptist*, or *Midsummer* (celebrated on the Saturday closest to 24 June). Like the Feast of Saint Lucy, this too is a celebration of light versus winter darkness. And tradition makes the Feast of St. John a night of magic. For example, it is believed that the dew which falls that night is a miraculous drug, or if you pick seven different species of flowers in seven different fields, tie them together and put the posy under your pillow you will see your future spouse in your dreams that night. Food, too, is an important part of the traditions: tables are laden with herring prepared in many different ways, new potatoes and strawberries. Like all people who enjoy the company of friends and a drink or two, Swedes love their food, and Swedish cuisine is the richest in all Scandinavia.

MORA

Mora, one of the most picturesque towns in the Lake Siljan area, was the birthplace of the famous Swedish artist, Anders Zorn. In addition to a museum dedicated to his works , the town is known for its lumber mills, metal working and as a winter-sport resort. Dominated by the majestic contours of the thirteenth century *church* that is topped by a XVII century tower, Mora also owes part of its fame to the fact that it is home of an important historic celebration, the **Vasaloppet** (the Vasa ski race). In March of each year, several thousand cross-country skiers gather here for the 88.8 km long race over the same route that Gustav Vasa covered in 1521 to rouse the valley folk to fight against the Danish King Christian.

The church in the town of Mora. Below, the area's typical crafts, with the horse that has become the symbol of Sweden. Opposite page, shots of the world's most famous cross-country skiing race, the Vasaloppet, and two "trophies" from the museum dedicated to this historic event.

ANDERS ZORN

Born at Utmeland, in the vicinity of Mora in 1860 Zorn studied art in Paris. He maintained close ties with his native Sweden and soon gained a strong reputation as an engraver and painter who drew his inspiration from genre scenes of Swedish country life. One of his most famous sculptures is the *statue of Gustav Vasa* that stands in Stockholm. Anders Zorn deeply loved his home and its old traditions: he died at Mora in 1920.

THE BIRTH OF A WOODEN HORSE

One of the most well-loved symbols of Sweden is the carved, painted *Dala horse*. The object dates back to the XVIII century when the woodcutters made toys for their own children. Today, this tradition still flourishes at *Nusnäs* near Mora. The wood comes from the forests around the Siljan and Orsa lakes, the animals are carved by machines, but they are decorated entirely by hand. In fact, after they are painted red, blue or black, they are decorated with motifs taken from the region's mural paintings.

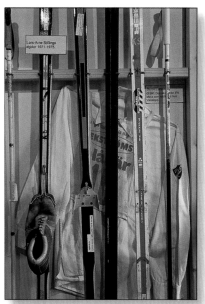

IN THE TRACKS OF GUSTAV VASA: THE VASALOPPET

The most popular cross-country skiing race in Sweden is the *Vasaloppet*. It is a roughly 90 km race from Berga to Mora and is open to men and women from around the world. It is held each year to commemorate the patriotic endeavor of Gustav Vasa in 1521 in the Dalarna district. He wanted to convince the valley dwellers to fight against King Christian of Denmark, but they were reluctant to follow his advice and instigation to rebellion so they initially denied him support. Therefore, Gustav Vasa put on his skis and headed towards the Norwegian border to continue his exhortations to revolt. He was overtaken by two men, sent by the people of Mora, who begged him to turn back, but in the meantime the townspeople had changed their minds. The route Vasa traveled to Mora is more or less the same as the trail of the *Vasaloppet* today. Thousands of cross-country skiers compete in this race which is held on the first Sunday in March every year. This historic event was first held in 1922, sponsored by the journalist Anders Pers, and there were 119 skiers. Currently over 12,000 compete each year.

A LOOK AT THE WILDLIFE

A country that has always respected the environment – even before it became fashionable to do so – Sweden with its 25 national parks and 1400 natural reserves has an extremely varied and interesting wildlife population in spite of a climate that guarantees long, cold and snowy winters. Obviously, the climate has affected the animals that have chosen Sweden's immense open spaces as their habitat. The snow-filled woods abound with lynxes, wolves, bears, Arctic foxes, otters and wolverines or gluttons as well as a ruminants such as deer, roe deer, elk and of course, in addition to musk ox, the reindeer that dominate the northernmost lands. There are also countless species of birds, both non-migratory and migratory, from cranes to swans, to marsh birds, especially on the islands of Öland and Gotland. And then there are the waters, the rivers, lakes and sea in a country where fishing is a national hobby, and they offer an extraordinary variety of fish, including salmon and then…there are the whales!

TÄLLBERG

In a truly delightful setting, amidst age-old forests, on a peninsula that reaches into the waters of *Lake Siljan*, Tällberg is home to an unusual and interesting **Outdoor Museum** (*Holen hembygdsmuseum*).

Here, in old buildings we can admire the items that comprised the collections of the painter Gustav Ankarcrona (1869-1933), along with an extraordinary gallery of toys, tools and household items.

Picturesque wooden houses are typical of this area where everything "talks about" the famous horse that is the symbol of Sweden.

RÄTTVIK

Another typical village of the Dalarna district with its rustic wooden houses (some date back to the seventeenth century) and nearby *Lake Siljan*, plowed by the typical, locally built church-boats that are offshoots of Viking vessels, is Rättvik, a resort that is quite popular during the summer. The season hosts the *Folklore, Music and Dance Festival*. And this is no coincidence: Rättvik has a passion for sports, pottery and music. Dominated by the large thirteenth century church that was remodeled and embellished with frescoes, this charming village is also home to the ***Gammelgården,*** an *outdoor museum,* that features old houses, and craft items; the village lives in perfect harmony with its lake that, according to tradition, was formed when a meteorite fell to earth.

Images from the famous outdoor museum at Rättvik.

SUNDBORN: CARL LARSSON'S WATERCOLORS

The warm and magic atmospheres of Nordic homes with wooden floors and window frames, porcelain stoves, pastel colors and healthy, blonde children scampering about, were rendered with feeling, love and extraordinary talent by the Swedish painter, Carl Larsson (Stockholm 1853-Sundborn 1919)

His watercolors – famous throughout the world in reproductions – are displayed in the **Sundborn Museum** at Dalarna, once the artist's favorite place.

As cheerful as a doll's house, colorful and cozy, *"Lilla Hyttnäs,"* as his Sundborn house is called, was given to the artist by his father-in-law. Carl Larsson moved there with his wife in 1889 after completing his training around Europe.

In France, where he met the Impressionists, he embraced the *en plain air* technique and the use of watercolors. Upon his return to Sweden he became a supporter of the style, going against the official painting of the Academy that was devoted to historical and patriotic celebrations. Larsson found his original inspiration at Dalarna, and today we can admire his many paintings of familiar subjects – interiors, scenes from daily life as well as landscapes and farm scenes. The joyful, sunny side of the Swedish soul is revealed with all its magic in these paintings.

Delightful Sundborn and the charming house-museum (bottom right) of its most famous son, the painter Carl Larsson who drew his inspiration from the atmosphere of these places. Below, a self-portrait of the artist.

FATHER CHRISTMAS

Jultomte, the Swedish Santa Claus spends most of the year in the heart of the Dalarna district, among the frozen lakes in a large, snow-covered park at Tomteland. Here, with his countless helpers, the elves, he fills the thousands of requests for gifts that arrive from all over the world. There, in front of his delightful wooden house stands the majestic sleigh that reindeers pull to the homes of thousands of children awaiting his gifts on Christmas Eve. The interior of Santa's house is a magical dream: a big burning fireplace in the parlor, a bed with a rainbow-shaped canopy and a study overflowing with books, gifts and letters that come from all over the world. Upstairs, in a room that only children are allowed to enter, *Jultomte* tells wonderful stories in an enchanted atmosphere.

If you would like to visit or write to him, the address is:
TOMTELAND
Gesunda
790 43 Sollerön, Sweden

THE FEAST OF SAINT LUCY

As in many other Christian countries, Swedes have great Easter and Christmas traditions. However, they also have two very particular celebrations as well, the Feast of Saint Lucy and the Feast of Saint John the Baptist – or Midsummer.
The Feast of Saint Lucy is 13 December, which according to tradition is the shortest day of the year, in honor of the winter solstice.
On the morning of the 13th a girl, wearing a long white dress, a red sash and a crown of candles on her head goes through every office, house, school, corporation, and through villages and farms, offering ginger biscuits, saffron rolls, coffee and hot, spiced wine known as *glögg*.
In 1928 the *Stockholm's Dagblad,* one of the country's leading newspapers, launched a contest for the election of Stockholm's Lucy, and ever since then the Lucys are selected every year.
The candles they wear on their heads symbolize light defeating the evil forces of the night and winter in expectation of the return of light-filled spring days.

WALPURGIS FEAST

Celebrated on 30 April (*Valborgsmässoafton*) this is one of the most important feasts in all Sweden because it heralds the arrival of spring – even if the mild weather does not begin at the same time throughout the country. In fact, parts of Sweden are still covered with snow and the people continue to bundle up in furs and sweaters.

THE GREEN LAKELAND

Sweden is a country of strong colors: the dark green of the woods, the intense shades of the dawn and sunset, and blue – of the sea, the rivers, and in particular, the numerous, immense and magical lakes that are so characteristic of the entire country, especially the south. Frozen over in winter and a dark blue in the summer months, these splendid stretches of water, whether large or small, scattered with islands or edged with conifers, turn the land into an amazing lake kingdom.

GÖTEBORG

Like a blue ribbon, the *Göta Kanal* winds its way along 518 km connecting Stockholm to Göteborg, the nation's second largest city and the main port of all Scandinavia. Established by King Gustav II Adolf in 1621, the city owes the canal-structure to Dutch architects, and there are many sites and places that reiterate its maritime calling.

The first is the *Östindiska Huset,* the East Indies Company, founded by Dutch, German and Scottish merchants in the seventeenth century and now the **Historical, Archeological and Ethnographic Museum**.

The next place of interest is the *Sjöfartsmuseet*, the *Maritime Museum,* and then the fish market, the *Feskekörka*, always a bustling, lively place. The *Poseidon Fountain,* by Carl Milles, in the *Götaplatsen,* the city's business center, is a tribute to the riches and power of the sea. If the sea and sailors are the backbone of this elegant city's life, it is just as true that Göteborg is a lively cultural center and is very much attuned to artistic activities.

Above left, the statue of Gustav II Adolf, founder of the city; right, a view of modern Goteborg, with its futuristic buildings and sophisticated design. Below, the Göteborgs Utkiken, the 86 meter skyscraper that has become an authentic symbol of the city. The moored "Barken Viking," a ship that has been converted into a famous restaurant and hotel.

Not only is there a noteworthy **Museum of Fine Arts** (the *Konstmuseum*) with an important collection of Italian, Spanish and Flemish paintings and works from the Swedish and French schools from the XVII to the XX century, there is the **Museum of Applied Arts** (*Röhsska Konstslöjdmuseet*) and the *Antikhallarna,* the biggest antiques market in all Sweden.

When it comes to leisure and relaxation, there are theaters, cafés and nightspots galore, but above all there is the amusement park with a myriad of attractions at *Liseberg.*

From the top, the Poseidon Fountain, the exterior of the Konstmuseum, with a room on the left; the cathedral (right), and the Christinae Kyrka, built by Göteborg's German community on the banks of one of the many navigable canals that offer a closer and truer vista of the city.

MARSTRAND

North of Göteborg, the county of Bohuslän overlooks the sea with a jagged coastline of granitic rocks and small islets dotted with quaint fishing villages. Popular with tourists and characterized by a decidedly untamed environment, the area is also famous for its old fortresses. Among these is the *Carlsten Fästning*, the castle that dominates the town of Marstrand, a renowned beach resort as well as a top ranking sailing center. Here, where dozens of islets wink from the sea, skilled craftsmen have been handing down their fine traditions for centuries.

SMÖGEN

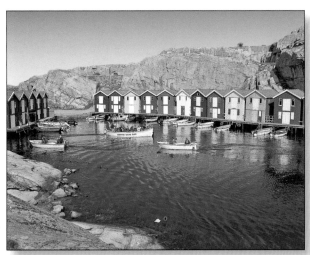

This picturesque island's economy is based on fishing – and primarily shrimp. Smögen is famous for its colorful houses that stand out brightly against the dark waters. But, it is only one of the many enchanting little islands, crowded with fishing villages and boats that dot the coast of Bohuslän province in southeastern Sweden.

Above left, the many attractions in the splendid country of Bohuslän in southwestern Sweden include mighty old fortresses.

Brightly colored wooden houses, so dear to Swedish hearts, facing the sea, the fishing boats and jagged islands paint an unforgettable landscape scene along the coasts of Bohuslän.

The fascinating archeological site at Tanum with rock carvings depicting scenes of hunts, fishing and daily life.

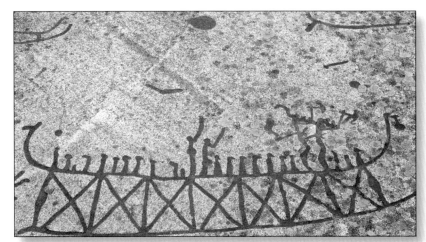

TANUM

If we reach Sweden from Southern Norway, we will be in what was the home of an ancient civilization with countless items from the Bronze Age and Viking Era. It is also a place where history and art blend with an enchanting landscape, amidst jagged coasts, many little islands and fields of heather. It is here that we find Tanum, an archeological site of exceptional value where *stone carvings* dating back to 3000 years ago have been perfectly conserved. Carved into the gray granite that is typical of the region, using stone tools these ancient images illustrate many aspects of life and society. Originally the carvings may have been tinted brown or ochre, with a special grease used to bind the colors. Today, red pigment rubbed over the carvings makes it easier to understand the subjects. There are many scenes with ships, humans (the women are recognizable by their long hair and the men by their pronounced sexual features), different types of animals and hunts.

SKARA

The seat of Sweden's first bishopric, in addition to being a lively cultural center where the country's fifth university (XVII century) was established, today Skara is the capital city of Skaraborg province, with an economy based on farming and food processing. So, it is no coincidence that it also has an unusual specialty: cherry fritters that are the object of a summer festival every year. The old city center is clustered around the massive **cathedral** that was built from wood in the XI century. Beneath its Romanesque towers the structure is Gothic as a result of fourteenth century modifications. The church was painstakingly restored after a disastrous fire in 1949, therefore it also has some very fine modern parts as well, such as the *stained glass windows* of the choir by Bo Beskow (1950) right near the ornate seventeenth century *altar.* Not far from here, an island in the huge *Lake Vänern*, is the home of the majestic **Läckö Castle** built by the bishops of Skara at the end of

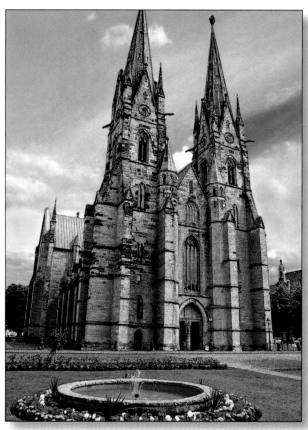

The soaring cathedral of Skara, a Gothic structure with Romanesque towers. Left, and below, the Läckö Castle and its splendid interiors.

the thirteenth century to serve as a pilgrims' hospice. Subsequently, it came under the ownership of the de la Gardie family, and today it is one of most beautiful stately homes in Sweden. Its elegantly frescoed rooms are often used to host art exhibitions, and there is also a lovely *chapel.*

VARNHEM ABBEY

A Cistercian *monastery* was built not far from Skara, at Varnhem, in 1143. It was destined to attain a power and splendor that Sweden had never seen before. However, it was the Reformation, warmly supported by Gustav Vasa that sealed its fate and led to its inevitable closing (1533). Only the Romanesque *church* survived the coming centuries as it was the majestic funeral chapel of the powerful de la Gardie family. Here, is the final resting place of Birger Jarl, the founder of Stockholm, who died in 1266.

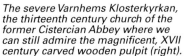

The severe Varnhems Klosterkyrkan, the thirteenth century church of the former Cistercian Abbey where we can still admire the magnificent, XVII century carved wooden pulpit (right).

Boats in the harbor and forests reflected in sparkling blue water:
this is the enchanted atmosphere of Lake Vättern.

LAKE VÄTTERN

The second largest in size, and located in the middle of Southern Sweden, Lake Vättern stretches north-south in a natural setting of rare beauty. Set among green valleys, little islands and heavily forested hills, this lake is known for the depth of its icy waters and its abundance of fish.

VADSTENA

The city of Vadstena stands on the eastern shore of Lake Vättern, in the Östergötland. The city was built around a XIV century abbey dedicated to Saint Brigitta. One of the highlights of the abbey is the *Blåkyrkan,* the **Blue Church**, that gets its name from the bluish hue of its stones. It is a Gothic structure with three elegant naves and it houses important paintings and sculptures from the Lubeck school, as well as the *tomb* of the saint. Not far from here, we can find the oldest piece of writing in Sweden, the **runic stone of Rök**. The ancient text it bears is the first piece of Swedish literature.

Another great point of interest in this picturesque city is the *Vadstena Slott*, an imposing Dutch style castle that dates from the Swedish Renaissance. It was the residence of Gustav Vasa who had it constructed as the city's fortress in 1545. Currently, it houses the Government Archives.

Above, the imposing Castle of Vadstena that conserves great masterpieces such as the Deposition *by Van Dyck and the* Portrait of Gustav Vasa, *as well as the priceless carved wooden Altar of the Rosary. Below, the magnificent Abbey Church.*

GÖTA KANAL

Carved between the vast green plains, this long and narrow strip of blue, with a complex system of locks is the *Göta Kanal* that links Stockholm and Göteborg. Winding its way through huge inland lakes, it is the culmination of a great Swedish dream. In fact, the idea of connecting the waters of the Baltic Sea to Lake Vättern, to facilitate the transport of lumber, food and goods was nurtured for centuries. But it was only in the first half of the eighteenth century that Karl XII ordered excavations to begin.

The work actually started in 1810, by order of Count Baltzar von Platen, who was also a government minister. It took over twenty years and enormous outlays

The Göta Kanal offers delightful cruises and an interesting tour through the heart of historic Sweden.

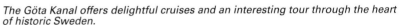

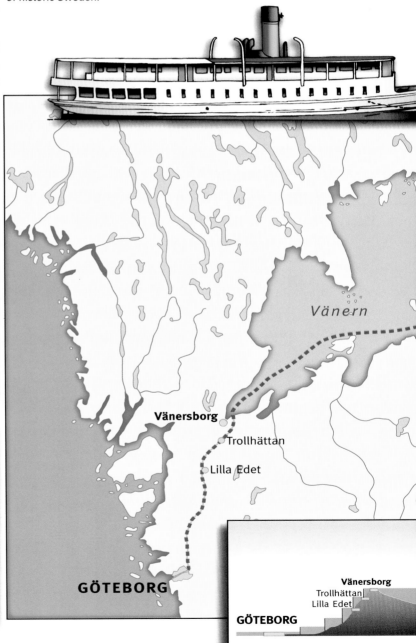

of money and manpower to complete the job.

By the time the canal was opened to traffic, it already had a fierce and efficient competitor: the railroad. However, it had no rivals in terms of charm and adventure and it has maintained its popularity up to the present with the many cruises (from three to five days) that are organized along its calm waters.

Boats and locks are two constant sights along the Göta Kanal.

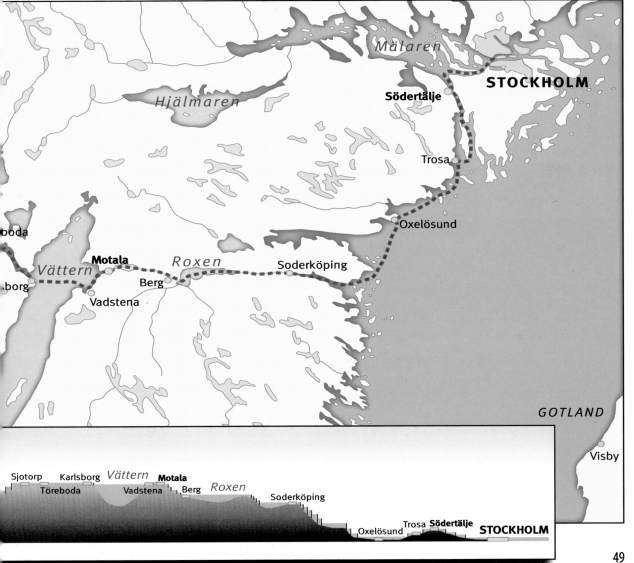

BETWEEN NATURE AND HISTORY

A land of ancient traditions and forests, of legends and untamed territories, Sweden has long been distinguished for its respect for nature and its jealous ties to its important history. For this reason, even the most common pictures of this country show old, majestic buildings together extraordinary views of a lush, powerful nature, the undisputed mistress of vast, empty spaces, capable of withstanding the rigors of northern winters to burst into late, but spectacular, springs every year.

MALMÖ

Sweden's third largest city and second ranking port is Malmö, that faces south and has regularly scheduled service to Copenhagen. An important city of the Hanseatic League and military stronghold, Denmark only ceded the city to Sweden at the end of the XVII century when the Peace of Roskilde definitely sanctioned the transfer.

Even though it is a city of business and industry, the "southern" atmosphere makes Malmö a cheerful, carefree place as we can see in its many restaurants, shops, nightspots and streets where business thrives. In addition Malmö is a very green city, with the huge *Limhamn park* that offers sports of all kinds and many other green areas. Echoes of the past can be heard around *Lilla Torget*, a small plaza with its old, square paving stones, surrounded by XVII and XVIII century frame houses. And there is another curiosity: Malmö is home to one of the biggest theaters in Scandinavia, the **Stadsteatern,** founded in 1944 with a seating capacity of 1700.

A futuristic feat of modern engineering starts from a suburb south of Malmö: the bridge over the Öresund. It is 7.8 km long (of which 1.09 km are suspended) and 57 meters high (to allow ships to pass beneath). It was opened on 1 July 2000 and continues with a 4.05 km. long island and a tunnel of the same length and connects Sweden to Denmark where the Copenhagen Airport is just a short distance away.

Lively, charming Malmö: above, the City Hall with the spires of the church of St. Peter in the background, below, Lilla Torget the delightful square bounded by eighteenth century buildings, and left, the railroad station.

LUND

For centuries the impressive bulk of the **cathedral** of Lund, in the lush, green province of Skåne was the first sight to greet visitors who approached the city. Established in 1080 by the Danish king, Canute the Saint, and consecrated in 1145, it is certainly one of the oldest archiespiscopal churches in Scandinavia and ranks among the most beautiful Romanesque buildings in all Northern Europe.

In addition to the *crypt* where famous Swedes are interred, the carved wooden choir stalls and altar, there is a fascinating XIV century *astronomical clock*. Every day at noon and three o'clock in the afternoon, the clock displays its fantastic works: knights engage in a duel, the organ plays *in dulci jubilo,* and tiny doors open for three miniature Kings in line to offer their tributes to the Virgin and Child.

The entire city of Lund emanates charm with its picturesque streets, the old market and the *Lundagård park,* where the red brick former royal residence was transformed into the university in 1666. Today, the structure is the *library* of the **university** which is second in importance only to Uppsala.

The 30,000 students enliven this southern city throughout the year, but especially during Walpurgis Feast on 30 April and the mid-May Carnival that is held every four years.

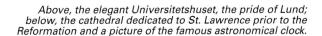

Above, the elegant Universitetshuset, the pride of Lund; below, the cathedral dedicated to St. Lawrence prior to the Reformation and a picture of the famous astronomical clock.

HELSINGBORG

For many visitors, Helsingborg is their first point of contact with Sweden. In fact, those who arrive from Denmark, leave behind Hamlet's castle at Helsingor to take one of the many ferries that make the 4.5 kilometer crossing that separates the two countries. Already a major European city in the XVII century, Helsingborg was long an object of rivalry between Denmark and Sweden because of its strategic, dominant position on the Baltic Sea.

Today it is mainly an industrial city that does conserve important vestiges of its past such as the *Kärnan Tower* and the beautiful **Church of Saint Mary** (*Sankta Maria Kyrka*). The Gothic style, plain brick structure owes its importance and artistic value to the interior and extraordinary decorations. The highlights are the *pulpit*, the *baptismal font*, the huge *chandelier*, two *stained glass windows* and the XV century German *altarpiece*.

The docking point for the big ferries that provide daily service to Denmark, Helsingborg is a modern harbor with a long, long history. It is a sparkling destination for Danes who want to shop.

Views of the city: the Neo-Gothic Town Hall on the Stortorget, the Kärnan Tower and a glimpse of the port.

MÖLLE

Perched just a few kilometers from the tip of the rocky peninsula of *Kullen*, stretching into the icy waters of the Kattegat, and the nearby contours of the Danish coast, Mölle is a typical fishing village that dominates the entire west coast of Sweden. Here the sea and fishing are clearly the main economic resources, but the untamed environment, and the grottoes carved into the rock by the crashing waves are unusual, fascinating attractions.

Fishermen, fishing boats, fish, shellfish and the sea: this is the untamed world of Mölle.

ARILD

Not far from Mölle, set among the rocks of the same, picturesque peninsula there is another charming seaside town, Arild, with its small harbor and brightly colored houses that stand out against the deep blue of the Kattegat's waves and the bright green vegetation. One of the finest manmade sights in Arild is the historic **Church of Sankt Arild** that dates from the XII century.

Arild, charming houses nestled in greenery are just a short walk from a super, fish-filled sea.

THE CASTLES

Scania, the southernmost county in Sweden, with its fertile plains that earned it the name of "Sweden's breadbasket," stretches along the coast of a fish-filled sea. For centuries it was a treacherous breach open to invaders and other dangers. It was the area's prosperity and opulence that led to the construction of the extraordinary number of castles (there are about one hundred dotting the region) that served as lavish homes for powerful families. The constant need for defenses is the reason that the oldest ones are built more like impenetrable fortresses. If

*Above, the Renaissance Castle of Vittskövle.
Below, the majestic Castle of Sofiero.*

the elegant **Castle of Sofiero** (King Gustav VI Adolf used it as his summer residence and laboratory, enthusiastic botanist that he was) owes its graceful appearance to the fact that it is relatively "new," the same cannot be said for the Renaissance manor at **Vittskövle** (1553-1577). It is not far from Åhus, and is surrounded by large moats and a huge garden. The severe **Glimmingehus Castle**, on the other hand, is a mighty fortress, built in 1499, comprising several buildings, protected by walls and moats, with stepped roofs and narrow embrasures. It is the only Medieval Swedish castle that has survived intact to the present.

The forbidding looking old Castle of Glimmingehus seems to still live in the Middle Ages.

SWEDISH HOUSES

Even private homes in Sweden are a distinctive feature of the landscape as well as part of a great tradition. Nestled in greenery or perched on rocks overlooking the sea (like the typical *stuga*) or standing on low walls, they were built from wood, the most abundant construction material in a land rich in forests, and the most suitable for the rigors of northern winters.
Stone was gradually incorporated as a building material after the seventeenth-eighteenth centuries, but one feature never changed. The bright, lively colors are practically a way of bringing cheer to the long, dark Scandinavian winters.

Wooden houses, houses on the lakeshore, at the sea or on a picturesque cobblestone square, red, white or yellow houses that fit perfectly into the environment: this too, is Sweden.

SWEDISH FOODS

Combinations of sweet and savory flavors are typical of
Swedish foods. So, it is not unusual to come across meat
or fish dishes prepared with salt, sugar, spices, blueberries,
cream or apple sauce. The most famous Swedish meal
is the *smörgåsbord*, a lavish buffet with
nearly every kind of dish. Herring, prepared
in a myriad of ways, is a staple of the
smörgåsbord, along with marinated or
smoked salmon and sardines or eel, according
to the season. Crayfish deserve a word
apart, they are so popular in Sweden that
there is even a holiday in their honor. The
crayfish-fishing season begins on the second
Wednesday in August, and a few days later
people get together outdoors, wearing odd
caps and paper napkins set about feasting
on the shellfish that are becoming a rarity.
They are cooked with dill, served with bread
and cheese, and washed down with beer and
schnapps. As for meats, on the *smörgåsbord*
table you can find liver pâté, ham, steaks,
smoked reindeer, different kinds of meatballs
and sausages. Salads, cabbage, spinach and
mashed potatoes are the typical side dishes, and every self-
respecting meal ends with cheese. There is also a huge variety
of breads: with dill, white, and rye, but the distinguishing
feature is the oven-dried bread with a hole in the middle that
recalls the old tradition of farmers' kitchens where there was
a peg on which the loaves were stacked.
The main meal is in the evening, for lunch Swedes prefer
something quick and light. Restaurants generally serve
classic, home-style foods, such as the delicious local
crayfish, *pannkakor* which are different types of crepes,
rårakor, pork fritters, *pytt-i-panna* a stew made with eggs
and peas or *kåldolmar*, stuffed cabbage.
Goose is popular in the south, reindeer
and wood grouse are typical of the
North, while trout, herring and codfish
dominate in Central Sweden. Beer, on
the other hand, is drunk throughout
the country, especially Pilsner-lagers
in light, medium and strong brews, as
well as strong schnapps. As in many other
countries, the
sale of alcoholic beverages is subject to regulations: they
are not available before noon, except by the bottle in stores
with a *Systembolaget* sign. And you must be twenty to
purchase them. The huge variety of foods, cultural traditions,
customs, territories and peoples comprising Sweden present
themselves to visitors in a kaleidoscopic vision. At one end
there is the warm, cozy south and the lively stimulating
center; at the other the fascinating, mysterious silence of the
Great North, where, far from our chaotic civilization, we can
truly feel at one with nature.

HALLAND COUNTY

In the vast county that stretches south of Göteborg, Halland is remarkable for its extraordinary beaches that are favorite tourist destinations, and the splendid inland areas where, amidst the lush forests we find the important *Hallands Väderö* natural reserve.

In these areas, that have been inhabited since ancient times, especially in the vicinity of *Lake Lyngern,* we can admire *rock carvings* dating from the Bronze Age, and dozens of *menhirs,* the typical tombstones of the Iron Age that are scattered around the vast plains.

Lush, green forests, broad open plains and clear signs of an ancient past (like menhirs, ancient tombstones) characterize vast areas of Halland County.

BETWEEN FORESTS AND ETERNAL GLACIERS

If we exclude a tiny portion dedicated to farming (about 7% of the country's total land area) roughly 60% of Sweden is covered by thick, shady forests – mainly conifers – but farther south there are lush broadleaved woods. The rest of the country is barren with seemingly endless tundra reaching up to the Arctic through moors and bare rocks culminating in majestic glaciers.

BLEKINGE PROVINCE

A small county in south-eastern Sweden, Blekinge is famous for its forests
and inland waterways, for its sandy
beaches on the Baltic and for the
splendid archipelago – the southernmost in the whole country – of countless islands big and small.
Along the coast there is a chain of
enterprising cities as strongly linked
to history as they are to fishing: from
Sölvesborg to *Mörrum,* from *Karls-
hamm* – an historic market town, to
Ronneby, a fine spa town, to *Karlskrona.*

KARLSKRONA

Karlskrona, the capital of Blekinge
Province, is the second biggest port
and the main naval base in Sweden.
This aristocratic city comprises about
thirty islands connected by bridges. It
is also home to an interesting **Maritime Museum** that is famous for its
original architecture.

*Views of Blekinge and Karlskrona:
above, typical houses; left, one of the
city's charming squares.*

The Maritime Museum at Karlskrona has a very unusual home: it was created in the XVII century arsenal. Along with many interesting artifacts, the museum has an extraordinary collection of figureheads.

Kalmar Castle

One of the most famous and most beautiful fortresses in the whole country, the Kalmar Castle is still as mighty as ever with its walls, bastions and distinctively roofed seven towers. Erected in the XIII century it was more or less completely remodeled in the Renaissance style during the sixteenth century under orders from Gustav Vasa. For a long time it served as a royal residence and over the centuries it withstood many, difficult sieges. Today, this splendid manor-castle still boasts stupendous and lavishly furnished and decorated rooms and a very fine *chapel*.

Kalmar: left the austere, late seventeenth century cathedral; below, the famous fortified manor that defended the city from the XIII century.

KALMAR

Kalmar is the capital city of the Småland region. Along with the interesting Baroque style cathedral with its bronze decorations, the city boasts the old *fortress* which for a long time served as the border point with Denmark, when the Danes governed the south.

What was Sweden's oldest maritime city is now linked to *Öland Island* by a bridge that was opened in 1972 and for a long time held the record as Europe's longest bridge spanning 6,072 meters.

JÖNKÖPING AND SWEDISH MATCHES

In many languages the words "Swedes" are only the people of Sweden; in many others they are the *matches* that have been manufactured here since 1840. The several phases that led to the development of what is a commonplace item – but actually has a very fascinating history – are featured in the *Match Museum* in the city of *Jönköping* near Lake Vättern. Housed in the former factory owned by the brothers, Carl Frans and Johan Edvard Lundström, the first to have manufactured matches on an industrial scale, the museum traces the history of this absolutely common yet always useful item that was initially the object of complex chemical studies until the creation of *safety matches,* that in

turn became one of the significant products in the Swedish economy. Today, even the 14,000 labels of Jönköping matchboxes with their different subjects and colors are collectors' items. But, the museum is just one of the town's attractions – it is also the seat of the Court of Appeals of Southern Sweden. Jönköping still conserves many interesting seventeenth century buildings and has one of loveliest beaches of Lake Vättern right in the middle of town!

THE ART OF GLASSMAKING: BETWEEN TRADITION AND MODERN DESIGN

Among the many, many things about which Sweden can be truly proud, we cannot overlook its rich crafts which, combined with its unique design has created a perfect blend of the traditional and contemporary. Swedish crafts offer a range of internationally renowned wares from glassware to furniture to wood carvings – the famous *Dala horses* that have become a symbol of the whole country. Småland, and specifically the city of Nybro, are true "kingdoms of crystal and glass" carrying on with a tradition that has its roots in the sixteenth century. It was then that Gustav Vasa, with the help of master glassblowers who came from Venice, established the first glassworks in Sweden. The need for huge amounts of fuel soon forced the industry to move to an area with sufficient forest resources, that is wood, and iron-steel industries. The choice fell on Småland. With the advent of the eighteenth century glassmaking became industrial and led to the creation of firms that are still the pride of the Swedish economy: from the historic *Kosta glassworks* to *Rejmyre* to the younger, but still nineteenth century, *Orrefors* (founded in 1898).

VÄXJÖ

The "Crystal Kingdom" is located between the cities of Kalmar and Växjö, in an area of forests which, from the eighteenth century on were a source of fuel for the glassworks' furnaces.

Even today, more than 17 glassworks offer their original creations and give visitors an opportunity to watch the entire glassmaking process and to purchase items at better than retail prices.

For those who are interested in a full picture of this tradition, a visit to the **Småland Museum**, at Växjö is the perfect outing. The museum showcases over 27,000 glass items that document the development of the craft over the centuries along with the styles created by talented designers.

THE KOSTA GLASSWORKS

The ancient Egyptians already knew how to make glass as we can see from archeological finds datable around 2000 B.C.

The craft was brought to Sweden in the XVI century by Gustav Vasa who invited Venetian glassblowers to his court.

However, the first industrial scale glassworks in Sweden was established in 1742 in the heart of the area that can rightly be called the "Crystal Kingdom." And its brand, *Kosta*, created from the first two letters of the names of the founders, Anders Koskull and Georg Stahl, generals in the army of King Karl XII and later governors of the province, is still one of the finest names in glass and crystal today.

VIMMERBY

There isn't a child in the world who hasn't wanted – at least once – to enter the enchanted world of storybooks and meet the characters. Well, in Sweden they can. All it takes is a stop at Vimmerby in the province of Småland. The city dates from the Middle Ages and it was the home of one of the most important authors for children the world has ever known, **Astrid Lindgren**.

Just a few kilometers northwest of the city is **Astrid Lindgren World** the delight of thousands of children. Here is a miniature village with the most famous characters, houses and buildings created by this extraordinary writer.

Children can go in and out of the houses where "Rasmus," or "Ronja" or "Simon Small" lived, or run into **"Pippi Longstocking"** herself, or ride with "The Brothers Lionheart" or play with "Emil's" chickens, sheep and pigs and for one day enjoy the incredible thrill of being part of their favorite books.

For those who want a real storybook adventure, there is nothing better than a visit to the extraordinary village that is home of the Astrid Lindgren World.

ASTRID LINDGREN

One of the true great storytellers, beloved by children and adults throughout the world, Astrid Lindgren was born in 1907. During her long life (she died in 2002) she wrote more than 100 books for children that have been translated into dozens of languages and sold more

than 130 million copies worldwide. She created famous characters, from "Pippi Longstocking" to "Emil", just to mention two who are full-fledged members of Swedish – and not only Swedish! – traditions and loved by "children" of all ages.

ÖLAND ISLAND

Some people think of it as the realm of the winds, others like to remember its sun-drenched beaches and others yet, dream of the sunsets and endless horizons. All this is Öland, a fascinating and picturesque island where the Royal Family spends its summer holidays at the *Solliden summer residence*. 135 kilometers long and only 15 at its widest points, Öland is connected to the historic city of *Kalmar* by a 6,072 meter long bridge. Rich in history, the island conserves many Viking runic stones and Iron Age relics as well. One of the most interesting spots is the village of **Eketorp**, an archeological site dating from V century B.C. where brilliantly restored structures make it possible to gain an understanding of what life was like at the time. The Middle Ages, too, left their traces in the island's many churches, even if the true symbols of Öland are its *windmills:* there are more than 400 and they are protected national monuments. The only street that runs through the island from north to south traverses the *Stora Alvaret*, the Great Plain, a vast, treeless stretch, home to many species of flowers and stopping place for countless migratory birds and a true delight for ornithologists, botanists and people who simply love nature. And for those whose thoughts turn romantic at sunset, an outing to the island's southern tip and the *Långe Jan lighthouse* is bound to be unforgettable.

THE WINDMILLS

They may be in the Dutch or local style, but no matter, they have long done their job of helping out in the difficult work of farming the coastal lands of Öland. The giant wooden windmills, and especially the seven that stand in a neat row near *Störlinge* have become true symbols of this hospitable island with its warm sun and an extraordinarily mild climate.

Everything on Öland Island seems made to fit harmoniously into the environment, from the lighthouses to the elegant homes, from the old farmhouses – to which the Outdoor Museum at Himmelsberga is dedicated – to the mighty fortifications like Eketorps borg (above), the ancient fortresses of Ismantorpsborg and Gråborg.
Facing page, the Långe Jan lighthouse and the Palace of Solliden.

THE GOOD LAND

Gotland, literally the "good land" is the largest island in the Baltic Sea. This jewel of calcareous rock is a favorite destination of artists and statesmen (like the nearby *Island of Fårö*) thanks also to its sandy beaches and a paradise-like natural setting. The temperate climate has favored the development of lush vegetation with huge deciduous forests and different types of flowers including 36 species of orchids.

But, it is mainly for ornithologists that Gotland is a true paradise, with one of the richest groupings of birds in all Europe. In fact, there are 157 nest-building species that increase to 350 in spring. This important wildlife-naturalistic heritage is protected by 40 government controlled natural reserves on the island.

Once a Viking stronghold, later one of the most important centers of the Hanseatic League, over the centuries Gotland has played important roles as documented by the countless ruins and archeological sites that dot the island. More or less everywhere we can see mounds of stones from the Bronze Age, boat-shaped Viking tombs, churches and Medieval fortifications. And the most significant of these sites are at *Visby*, the capital of Gotland.

VISBY

Nicknamed the "city of the ruins and the roses," this historic town still has its walls that were built during the XIII-XIV centuries with a 3 km long battlement, 38 of the original 44 towers and 18 gates. Prehistoric, Viking and Medieval artifacts are set out to be admired in the **Gotland Fornsal,** a small local museum of great historic-artistic importance that houses exceptional items.

Several old churches – many in ruins – dot this charming Medieval town. Fortunately, the beautiful Romanesque-Gothic **Cathedral of Saint Mary**, built by German merchants, is in fine condition. The ruins of the *Church of Saint Nicholas,* serve as the setting for reenactment of the Medieval religious play, *Petrus de Dacia* by F. Mehler, during the yearly summer *Festival of Visby*. During the first week in August the city literally leaps backward in time: the population parades through the street in original period costumes. It is not uncommon to run into knights, merchants, ladies, witches and acrobats as we stroll through the streets. A thrilling tournament and elaborate historical pageant conclude the week of festivities.

The splendid natural context of Gotland Island – not by accident known as the Medieval Garden of the Baltic – is the perfect backdrop for the mighty walls that still offer protection, the splendidly conserved cathedral, the picturesque ruins of the Church of St. Nicholas that hosts religious pageants. The town of Visby has been declared an UNESCO World Heritage Site.

THE VIKINGS

The era of the Vikings in Sweden (800-1050 A.D.) was characterized by major eastward movements for purposes of trade and looting the areas along the Baltic Sea coasts and rivers that flow along Russia's plains.

Sailing on light, swift ships, until the IX century the Vikings established strategic outposts for trade such as *Rurik,* named for a Viking chief.

It was from his name that the vast plains surrounding Rurik "developed" into Russia and there the Vikings established the principalities of Novgorod and Kiev.

They went as far as the Black and Caspian seas where they traded with the Byzantine Empire and the Arabs. Significant testimonials of the period are the *bildstenar* (left), massive, figured stones decorated with Runic inscriptions commemorating a battle, a famous figure, or offering thanks to the gods.

On the Island of Gotland there are a great many figured stones with mainly geometric decorations that become increasingly complex with spiraling inscriptions and the earliest zoomorphic figures that later developed into what is known as the "Vendel style."

The *Uppland,* too, has an abundance of elaborate, figured stones with interlacing decorations that date from the final period of Viking migrations around the XI century. The same period has also left evidence of fine quality gold jewelry found in some Viking tombs.

ÖJA

Öja, a small, old hamlet, has a splendid **church** with elaborate bas-relief carvings above the portal. Inside are fine *fourteenth century frescoes* by the Master of the Passion; and a spectacular thirteenth century French ***Crucifix*** that is splendidly set between portrayals of the *Original Sin,* below and the *Hierarchy of Angels,* above.

Above, the portal and the magnificent Crucifix in the famous church at Öja. Below, the picturesque and uncontaminated Island of Fårö.

FÅRÖ ISLAND

This is a flat and solitary, small island of slightly more than 100 square kilometers. With its bare beaches, runic stones that are evidence of the Vikings, and a richly decorated Gothic *church* it has long been the favored hideaway of artists and statesmen – including the famous director Ingmar Bergman – who relish the paradisiacal seclusion it offers.

AT THE WORLD'S EDGE

In the northernmost part of Sweden, beyond the Arctic Circle are the boundless glaciers. Here winters continue without end, the summertime midnight sun glows softly and nature's contrasts are starkly accentuated. Meek pastures alternate with desolation or lush forests. Here is *Lapland*, sparkling white snow and the harshness of an adventurous life. The people have adapted to living in towns or villages which are now fascinating and innovative tourist destinations.

JÄMTLAND

A former possession of Norway, this beautiful and uncontaminated northern area stretches around crystalline *Lake Storsjön*. The city of **Östersund**, built by Gustav III at the end of the eighteenth century is famous for its *music festival*, held in summertime, of course. *Frösön Island*, the first settled area, the *Tännforsen Waterfalls* and the *Jamtli park-museum* are well worth a visit.

ÅNGERMANLAND

This county in northeast Sweden overlooks the Gulf of Bothnia. It is a very green region characterized by countless coastal towns (for many, many years the sea was the only avenue of communication in an area of impenetrable forests) and is famous for the rocks and rocky islands that create the spectacular **Höga Kusten** (*High Coast*) that is typical of this part of Sweden.

THE NORRBOTTEN REGION

A land of lakes and fiords, rivers, forests and mountains, the untamed Norrbotten, at the northeastern tip of Sweden was long a border territory, that is while Finland was part of Russia. Here we find the easternmost city of Sweden, **Haparanda**, as well as fortresses such as nineteenth century **Boden** – erected for defensive reasons and still the headquarters of an army garrison, and the interesting *Garnisonmuseet*, a museum dedicated to the last four centuries of the country's military history. But Norrbotten is also the land of hardworking industrial cities, such as lovely **Luleå** that was literally moved to the coast from inland during the middle of the XVII century to further its development and trade. There is an interesting nineteenth century *cathedral* and slightly further on, in the *Gammelstad* – the "old city" – the splendid Gothic church *Nederluleå*, nestled in a "city" of 425 little wooden houses formerly used by worshippers with a long way home. *Gammelstad*'s church-city is on UNESCO's world-heritage list.

LAPLAND

The midnight sun and the aurora borealis, peacefully grazing reindeer herds, going beyond the Arctic Circle and even further north among eternally snow-covered mountains and tundra that never thaws completely, not even in summer – these are just some of the fascinating wonders of Lapland. This is the northernmost part of Sweden bordering on Norway and Finland. Extraordinarily rich in minerals and characterized by harsh winters, crisscrossed by long roads and precious rail lines it is the land and realm of the Laps. The land is dotted with picturesque villages with austere huts and warehouses all built from wood. All around there is demanding and fascinating Nature– and she has allowed these areas to open to a new and important experience: gradual, yet respectful and rigorously controlled tourism.

Below, a classic village in cold Lapland; right, the peak imprisoned by the Kebnekaise glacier, the highest massif in Sweden rising to 2,111 meters.

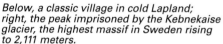

THE SAMI

The *Sami* people have lived in Lapland for ever. With their brightly colored – and warm – clothing and tenacity they have successfully challenged the long winters and freezing Arctic winds for millennia. They are nomads by calling and by choice, and are jealous of their ancient traditions that include a unique language and mythology. And they share their lives with their wonderful sled dogs. The Sami have just one, precious and irreplaceable resource: reindeer – their priceless wealth.

Between the rigors of long winters, the precarious nature of a traditionally nomadic life, the tough lifestyle, the most frugal shelters, the existence of the Sami people, who maintain very strong ties with their age-old customs, may seem filled with difficulties. They live in harmony with untamed nature and their most loyal companions, the reindeer, their only wealth. Originally raised for meat, today they are a fascinating and innovative tourist attraction, which makes them a new and precious economic resource.

ICEHOTEL: A HOTEL BELOW ZERO

Near the city of *Kiruna*, the main city in Swedish Lapland, in the village of *Jukkasjärvi*, the people built a hotel out of ice and snow. It is known as *Icehotel* and is the fruit of the brilliant imagination of Inge Bergqvist the head of the tourist village of Jukkasjärvi. In 1991 he began constructing the first, 60 square meter, section using an aluminum base structure and pressing snow on it. When the snow froze the aluminum template was removed leaving a perfect ice-room. Year after year construction became more complex until 1994 when, with the cooperation of the architect Aimo Räisänen, the building became a real hotel with dining room, bar, cinema – with an ice screen, church with a baptismal font carved from ice and an art gallery. The spacious bedrooms – all frozen and decorated with transparent ice carvings - are equipped with all "mod cons" including TV and stereo systems. There is no heating and the indoor temperature is always around -2/3° C, while outside it can drop to as low as -35°C. Guests come equipped with thermal clothing and sleeping bags – the beds are all covered with reindeer skins. Naturally the *Icehotel* closes – or rather melts away – in spring to be rebuilt differently each November.

Breathtaking views of the Icehotel, the glacier and Stora Sjöfallets National Park.

INDEX